Every Day, They Became Part of Him

poems by

Clark A. Pomerleau

Finishing Line Press
Georgetown, Kentucky

Every Day, They Became Part of Him

Copyright © 2023 by Clark A. Pomerleau
ISBN 979-8-88838-225-7 First Edition
All rights reserved under International and Pan-American Copyright Conventions. No part of this book may be reproduced in any manner whatsoever without written permission from the publisher, except in the case of brief quotations embodied in critical articles and reviews.

ACKNOWLEDGMENTS

Wordgathering: A Journal of Disability Poetry and Literature first published
    "Autopsy," "Borrowed, Faded Memories," "Bowl and Pitcher,"
    "Burst," "Chants All Over," "Disappear," "Every Day, They Became
    Part of Him," "Hole," and "Vapors' Cold, Crashing Balm."
"Spin" was first published in Ona Gritz and Taylor Carmen Savath, eds.,
    Welcome to the Resistance: Poetry as Protest (Galloway, NJ: South
    Jersey Culture & History Center, Stockton University, 2021).
"Bowl and Pitcher" and "Pine Needles Fall" appear in *About Place Journal*.
Beyond Queer Words published "Fission, Fusion, and Matter" in their
    December 2021 anthology.
"Appearances" and "Namesakes" first appeared in *Poached Hare*.
"Old Growth" first appeared in *Coffin Bell Journal*.

Publisher: Leah Huete de Maines
Editor: Christen Kincaid
Cover Art: Clark A. Pomerleau
Author Photo: Clark A. Pomerleau
Cover Design: Elizabeth Maines McCleavy

Order online: www.finishinglinepress.com
        also available on amazon.com

Author inquiries and mail orders:
Finishing Line Press
P. O. Box 1626
Georgetown, Kentucky 40324
U. S. A.

Table of Contents

Dedication and Inspiration

Acknowledgements

1. Him

Bowl and Pitcher 1

Loaf 2

Spin 3

The First Braid 4

Sharp 5

Tricky Questions 6

Appearances 8

Wonder 9

Rebirthright 10

Family Reunion 11

Fission, Fusion, and Matter 13

Poet of Earth 14

Witness 15

2. They

Cormorant Folktale 19

Namesakes 20

Hole 21

Shoshin 22

Borrowed, Faded Memories 23

Disappear 24

Wild Turkeys 25

Augury 26

Yearning Gaps 27

Guardian of Memory 28

Haunting 29

  Grey 30

  Resigned 31

3. Of

  Gecko Tail 35

  Violets 36

  Old Growth 37

  Precious Lineage 38

  1980s Specter 39

  Southern Medusa 40

  Now Ripe 41

  Sacral Adoptees 42

  Patron Catherine 43

  Clinging Dream 44

  Gather the Deck Again 45

  Burst 46

  Spirit Cove 47

4. Part

  Fly Away Dreams 51

  Felled 52

  Vapors' Cold, Crashing Balm 53

  Grief Work 54

  Autopsy 55

  Braid: I Learned from Dementia that I Could Not Stay 56

  For Life Anew 57

  Cicadas 58

  Pine Scent 59

  Rise 60

  Pine Needles Fall 61

  From Ash 62

  Babble 63

5. Every Day

- Listing Along 67
- Reflects 68
- Where Are the Squirrels? 69
- To Reason with My Crooked Cap 70
- Wintering Days 71
- Cloud Koan 72
- Cracks 73
- In Constellation 74
- Sounds behind the Traffic 75
- Gray Frosted into Elegance 76
- Sand 77
- Nature's Shield: a protection prayer 78
- Out of This World 79

6. Became

- Dandelion Seeds 83
- Sweet Flags from Disbanded Leaves 84
- Shut Down that Winter Home 86
- Cobalt Night Skies 88
- Hindsight Rebirthing 89
- Braid: He Wears Woods 90
- Insecurely Tethered 91
- Chants All Over 93
- Make My Man Basalt 94
- The Art of Dying 95
- Braid: Shrinking 96
- Fireweed 97
- Every Day, They Became Part of Him 98

Author Biography

With love to my family, subsequent mentors, and the "complementary fruit bowl" ripening in and after graduate school. Special gratitude for those who accompanied me through my mother's death from dementia.

A line from Walt Whitman's "There was a Child went Forth" inspired this collection. The poems in this volume center a character who absorbed lessons from family, educators, queer-trans folx, nature, and spirituality. That child went forth to fulfill his dreams and returned intentionally to help with elder care. Relationships braid together human joys and grief with mortality that reflects something bigger than us. Our protagonist's experience helps him navigate in a space where time no longer seems to move forward. He knows that celebrating the nature of queer and trans existence can initiate us into wonder. How do queer development, desire, and resilience open us to possibilities? What do trans perspectives reveal about natural, spiritual, and cultural dimensions? How can these perceptions support relating to a loved one with dementia?

1. Him

Bowl and Pitcher

Black basalt
was once molten
flowing fire
that scorched earth
before firming to bedrock
foundation the river carved
until people saw
a bowl and pitcher

Water pulls at the old soul part of me
rolling, sweeping, flowing
rivers call out
if I wade, I become another rock
or felled limb
the water goes around

Rocks sing
beyond our frequency
we know because
ground stones
turned in blower's hands
fuse glass that rings

I am drawn to the ground
that nourishes plants
and lulled by rhythmic water
powerful persistence
beneath its slip sliding ways

First, though, was fire
then the air
cooling into life

Loaf

Past a breath
Abyss
Dotted with suns
Multitudes of worlds
Beyond knowing.

Imagination unmoored
Flies through space
Travels as a body rests
Loaf with me and
Create unseen wonders.

Spin

Drifting toward sleep
when no one points out each body twitch
form floats up
turning an expanding specter.

By day, spinning displaces
jerks. Spirit free from every sniff
crack and stretch tallied as mad.
Joyful axis forces away melancholy.

That's why Wonder Woman's twirl
still thrills forty years after
homemade gold cuffs with red stars.
She taught me not to cram myself into a phone booth.

Some shadow part tried to shield me
before I knew myself reflected in queer tic kin
whispering, *The body is not destiny* until
I remade myself.
I flesh out, spin toward joy.

The First Braid[1]

To climb and play with boys every day
I braided my hair back from my face.
They grudgingly allowed I was good enough.

They admitted that I was as good
'Cuz I was their tenacious ideas man
Folding everyone in with kindness and fun.

Enfolding everyone in kindness and fun
I didn't care that some laughed daily
When I tucked the braid under Dad's olive cap.

I tucked hair under Dad's army cap
Until another boy asked to buy it
But I wouldn't sell my habit.

I wouldn't sell out my kin's customs—
Forbearer tomboys, baby dykes, and trans boys
Who climbed and played with cis boys every day.

---

[1] The Braid is a form that reappears in this volume. To Braid: Make 3 to 5 stanzas of 3 lines each. Each line has 9 to 11 syllables. The first line, or a variation of it, is the last line. Stanzas 2 and on take their first line from a line in the stanza above that has not been repeated (and is not the first line of the poem). It likely is strongest to repeat or vary the third line as the first line of the next stanza. Each stanza then adds two new lines. The Braid form is indebted to Jericho Brown's Duplex form in *The Tradition* (Copper Canyon Press, 2019). He explains the Duplex in "From the Archive: Pulitzer Prize Winner Jericho Brown's 'Invention,' *Poetry Foundation* (May 2020), (https://www.poetryfoundation.org/harriet-books/2020/05/invention: accessed 8 Nov. 2021).

Sharp

He sharpened my tongue
as a weapon against bullying.
Tuned my timbre to ring
with shrewd contempt if attacked.
We are small but cunning
with quick minds
language is our strength.
Pointed to skewer
and cut you down
to the nothing you are.
I was tender and needed to parry
in defense.
Then.

Tricky Questions

Earth turns her face to shun
her wistful sun
opening to off-black.
To what end?
Fitting my gaze to chronicle the scene
exceeds natural law.
While I wait for pupil slits to widen
at the glow of trees
index fingers poke upward
rubbing sides before wagging
Where, where?
Into near abyss coyotes pitch deeper questions
that saturate the skies.
Bones they divined with—
licked clean of marrow—
produced no offering.
The tricksters have scrabbled
to scratch down the stars
as captive audience for their constant queries.
They sing honest lines with uncommon gusto
fitted to varied breath
free from rulered rhyme
full of sublime emotions.
Displaced heavenly bodies sink into torpor
barely hearing the persistent upspeak?
The dimming nightlights yawn indifferent
whether plants become torches
with their borrowed light
or darkness reigns.
Threaded around trees and ferns
gleams a grounded trail
slime for marching on stomachs.
Slugs are faster plodders
than their walled-in cousins.
They form a double-time parade
far from salt-wielding slaves to an aesthetic hierarchy of beings.
But mollusks are not quick enough to evade prodding claws.

Running always fails.
Retracting leaves a target.
Foul slime or amputation may misdirect.
Shaken with insistence,
slugs expel answers
first chewing on the problem
of whether gifted apophallation would appease.
They spit out intersex multitudes
the why of their existence complete
with continuation and food to eat.
Forecasting eggs glisten,
nuggets of light for the spending.
Numinous replies
read the tea of brimming souls.
Too much for some.
Cryptic answers:
No paltry catalogue distills our essence.
The broken mends with concentrated effort
and something new.
Death, the true apex predator, may gum at life
but cannot consume it.
Gastropods know art is not science
How could anyone quantify awe?

Appearances

Like an empty bottle of eau de parfum
long ago brought from Quebec City
or the pea soup and gumbo from roux
immigrant tongues knew like trilled Rs
faded sense memories don't reach
across divides
of those who would not touch
on what they left.

Mom memorized enough French
to pass and make her teacher
veut la jeter par la fenêtre.[2]
Dad and I, eager pupils
recited to ghosts.

So, Mom cooked from
scentless English books
never traveled so far North or South
until I begged for crumbs of identity
left in Toronto and New Orleans.
Dad wanted too,
and showed us home.

In the black and white photo
from Waterville that I finger
Dad, Grandpa, Pépé remain
reflected in me
illustrate how I appear
as boy, father, sage.

---

[2]The teacher said, "And I could just throw you out the window" with frustration that Mom did not apply herself.

Wonder

That you are made of star stuff
is remotely true
but what specifically makes you you?
Your people, land, and experiences
braid together your world view.

We wonder how and why
stand outside in awe
whether looking at big sky
or out at the seas
across plains and fields
or at a forest of trees.

Rebirthright

Born wrong to *souvenir*
I dove right into past life
when present denied
murky future.

Ethereal Gallic tales
refuse mementos.
Journey delayed
sees a blood stranger
maid of Lorraine
nowhere to be found,
diffused as Jean d'Arc's last gasp.

Failed retellings
heritage ghosts
pulse lost stories.

But heat squeezed stones moan secrets.
Rivers course Native names
though cold makes that a listless chore.
They gasp sharp edge air
burble cadences
jut to the surface.

Grit, water, blood
mix an ink to
overwrite conqueror's scripts
until inflection rings with old truths
without concessions.
Revise to rebirth to birthright
redrawing the boundaries
back to dawn days radiance.

Family Reunion

Ease out of coastal work
two hours to wind down SR-3
past farms cut from forest
ocean pooled into lakes and ponds
roadside grass and groves
scanning for wildflowers.

Family reunion is always deeply interior
sunny, green, peace…through silence.

I pick a bouquet for Lorraine
yellow Black-eyed Susans, purple Vetch,
white Daisies and Queen Anne's Lace
for joy denied.

Past Mémère's house I go
self-conscious
in another shiny rental with away plates.
Because Grandpa married out
left behind, mouais?
Slow turn up the gravel drive
of an old French neighborhood.

Matriarch Marie married a mover
who left one river for another
across an imaginary line.
Grocer siring butchers and fishmongers
and a local naming tradition.
Surrounded by Maries et Josephs
le petit bébé Marie Emma et jeune Joseph John
beside Mémé (Marie) and Pépé (Joseph).

Tell me about taking Dad to Perry's Nut House
on the way to stock seafood for summer sale.
Little spitting image everyone knew
through generous, bon vivant Pépé,

We will laugh over Mom's disgust at
plates and chowder
from Young's Lobster Pound
food that looked too much alive.

Silent that you set Grandpa's wage so low
Grandma could not pay the heating bill.

I always pack garden gloves and pruning snips
to tidy the yard before showing you the flowers
and taking a grassy seat across from you.
Only the trees whisper that Lorraine
has finally returned in the end
from her wandering husband
doomed to be underfoot.
We sit in silence.

Grand-tante, I will tell your sister I saw you
when I drive through the woods.
I've cleaned and put flowers on your plaque
because you did not get a headstone.
You always wanted to be like her.
Her grave marker awaits at Mt. Mercy.
She is sharp and well
maybe the best among the innocents.

Fission, Fusion, and Matter

Reincarnation without
The barrier of time
A story for the ages.
Fission for a future
Where everything includes
A spark and heat.
Within me, internal suns
Robust soil, crashing oceans
Fuse with the same everywhere
Inherent worth
Needs outward expression
Matter matters in our
Sensory world.
Through cracks I have burst
Hardened, weathered
Nurtured a lush Green Man
I tend to like my men clean-cut
And my mountains old growth.

Poet of Earth

Poet of Earth
who taught us to see the thrush
singing in the lilac
smell sweetness
on the breeze
and pungent scent
on the workmen
as worthy of a longing gaze
as your soldier boys
and streetcar desires

Poet who walked the earth
in American cities
drawn exceptionally
for their promise
in the process of becoming
who listed everything
democratically
who put me in
my body
myself
my country

Who followed the swallow
the river
the shoreline
to a new vantage
over the same land
worthy of
an American bard at last
to sing chants democratic

Witness

How do we witness all the world's suffering
and experience all the Earth's beauty
Not turn so sharply from sentient pain
that we miss wonder filled life

So many black hole elegies threaten
to swallow the numinous
Yet a moral imperative demands
we not absorb only what pleases

When extremes leave us speechless
like the wind knocked out
We gasp to re-inflate lungs
ineffable witness to everything

2. They

Cormorant Folktale

Every ripple seems to glow
as sunlight sparkles on the ocean's flow.
Cormorants bob with the wave
like buoys the ship to save.
I shield my gaze from silver glisten
and strain my ears to listen;
while sunning his outspread wings
a black envoy for my dead sings.
As dark birds come ashore to preen
lost loved ones return to be seen,
and so, I meet the butcher at the shore
whose face reflects mine more and more,
who tells me of our shared past
'til the sun sets and he fades at last.

Namesakes

From birth, foreordained to
stoke family's memories
your body the tie that binds them to
their past.
Called to replicate the original,
relative delight at specters
in your expressions, embodiment.
Double jeopardy should spirit fail—
disappointment in brother
dulling the shine of their golden boy.

Do elders see their ghosts in you?
Does their character seep in through
shared name?
What of bearing their tale is
about you?

Perhaps inspiration for continued, directed growth.
Remembering the dead,
honor the living.
Libations to ancestors.
Call the names.
Guidance across generations.

Hole

Father son stony blocks
veins of anxiety under the surface
as I drive to minor emergency.
The deadweight arm revives
in the waiting room.
A mini-stroke's effects gone
without reason.

Mom asks Dad
How is it going?
He slides off his chair.
Stop it!
The straight man is not miming.
Doctors find the hole in his heart.
We plunge in.

Shoshin

Feet crunch pea gravel
Slip back a fraction from a shiny
Bright red goal
Skidding onto wooden planks
To play a percussive octave
Dash back and forth

Running mind remembers
The red bridge as
Play, outing, family
Looping back to those
Seated
Time has weathered all
To silver

The view spans water
Fanning out from the falls
Slow to stop
Pooled water mirror
Breaks into concentric circles
As koi surface to swallow
Unwary water striders

Busy brain, tapping feet
Turn back to rushing falls
Balance on slippery wet stones
Meant to concentrate energy
Decelerate mind
The return to this manicured garden
Is a pilgrimage to see again

Borrowed, Faded Memories

A sensory fog of faded memories
punchy wisps that elude organizing
the soup of stories Mom served
molded a toddler mind.

Surprising how much past we borrow.
Dad's mental records still help me fact-check myself
while my aunt has archived tales of his forgotten youth.
It has been this way for generations.

Pooling recollections like scarce provisions
Dad knows names and histories of Mom's friends
whom he never met.
His mind holds the library of her life.

More and more she needs him to fill in the blanks.
They have intertwined their stories so long
he can find her words, finish her thoughts, and remember
for her.

Disappear

Growing up, we three had so much to say.
Everyday news; novel ideas; classic ruminations.
Repetition was an imposition on scarce time.
Exasperated, you would complain,
You already told me that.
I've heard that story before.
A childhood of dinner conversations,
an adulthood of weekly phone calls
…of not sharing the phone, so you wouldn't get stuck
on repeat.

I hear your tone in my impatience.
I want to go faster, cover more ground, exchange big thoughts.
I would settle for practical advice.
I yearn for pieces.
Meanwhile, despite whatever grumbling,
you stored away those stories to gnaw on
as you watch your love disappear.

Wild Turkeys

Like marauding hordes, the turkey rafter
invades the land daily. They take what food
they please, fill the road, stopping all comers.
A few used the patio as a runway
to perch safely on pine boughs at nightfall.
Now fourteen birds flock together, a stone;
not that many trees stand since the felling.
The man tires of fowl and of their shit.
He eyes them, craving Thanksgiving.
But the woman exclaims each time they appear.
They spur her tales of moose, coyote, deer,
her histories bereft of nouns or verbs
that make her the hushed Echo of her past.

Augury

Heron bright across grey heights
Beauty bounding out of sight.
Somberly replaced as vultures amass
to perch on roof, branch, mailbox, grass.
They converge around a possum
to feast on roadkill flotsam.
Fly toward my rooftop
and circle back as I take stock.
This is no augury.
It is not all about you or me.

Yearning Gaps

Does Golem's now-self-generated clay
patch the streets and repair cracked roof tiles?
Created now creating—
perhaps a spiraling gift.
Can she plug yearning gaps too?
I wish I could share a meal with you both.
Then help throw back the curtains and scour the messes
so the sun reaches calm corners.
Its cleansing rays bend to future lifetimes.
This will all happen again.
I wonder how different it will be
and how the cycle will refashion our bond.
I wish I could remember with equanimity.
But I feel too much of this life.
Bogged down in this being.
Golem, transform this quicksand
into a smoother supporting path.
I did not summon you; you owe me no fealty.
We just will trudge through,
scrape off the grit,
and apply it to the next muddle.

Guardian of Memory

Oh Stoic turned martyr, so removed from your love, what will you do now?
Metron as broken as Demeter in the winter of her days
Now sweet, now stymied through the haze.
Guardian of Memory
Nearly alone in the abyss
While the muse child visits
But only by seasons
Unauthorized to speak
Unable to quench thirst at the river of Memory.
And so, the cycle continues uninitiated.

Haunting

Sixteen-sunned belle
appears to me daily
haunting the hall.
I never knew you
a vision far removed.

You aged beyond romantic ideal
into the matriarchal triptych
and lived past your daughter's failed paint-by-numbers
into your son's cluttered landscape.
Thick oil connects us
I muse as I long to feel
the worn-smooth thumbhole of Granny's palette.
The vanishing point is on the horizon.

How would Granny paint you now
framed in the doorway
waiting for me to come and go.
She couldn't summon the
bittersweet
in her idealist style.

Grey

Wholly overcast
depopulated path
along standing water
with intermittent dead-ends
at civilization
backtrack into the prairie
peopled by dragonflies,
grasshoppers, crickets,
butterflies, bumblebees,
Seussian pods and fruits,
sunflower-like weeds
who brighten the grey
and enliven the morass.

Resigned

From your shoulders
ground dizzyingly far
I delighted in touching the ceiling.

On your back
safe hugging your neck
you could walk forever.

When you taught me to throw,
you were a great athlete
barely out of your prime.

When I was beyond mine,
you recalled having resigned yourself
always to be picked last.

I'm the younger you
grown melancholy with age
but not yet stoic.

3. Of

Gecko Tail

a lump of flesh
draws attention
as it spasms

a magician's redirection
during sleight of hand

What we don't see
is a matter of death throes
and regeneration

Violets

crushed violets between magnificent thighs
stained on sheets to dearest beloved

sex obsessed men examined leaves to
deflower us, de-story us, cut us down to pathologies
tiny men strove to minimize our love as sinful crazy crimes
cast out of polite society and heaven
driven underground

for how could invert homosexual pervert queers
ever reach the heights
We Did
through melancholy and strife
We Did

persistently we stole space for furtive intimacy
magnificent house parties paid rent
we held phenomenal faggot balls
performed a Cuban bride at Club My Oh My
found kindred preachers who married us
in tuxes and gowns not made for either of us

organized into reconstructed pride
built up tension through friction
until We Burst
We are Everywhere
no sermons, neglect, offensives
will stuff us snuff us out of sight

you say there is no stable
timeless We
I see / parameters recalibrate
but around the strategically essential imaginary
powerful center will always be

a whiff of violet
and magnificent thighs

Old Growth

Old growth canopy
dense enough
to snuff out seedlings
ancients hoard gold

rays cannot trickle down
then or now
but blame the young
for failing to thrive

We choked out
gangly pale
wait for
the ax to fall

Or fiery bolt strike
that flames lick
away leaves
revealing our patch of light.

Precious Lineage

Mary Magdalene retired to Provence
rich off all those men's failings
between surreptitious flings with her princex of peace
precious balance of feminine and masculine.
Freed to live openly, she
brought out her hommasses, dandies, epicenes
named Martha, Mary, or Matty for eons.
Our lavender lineage springs
from wine-watered fields.
Bathed in azure-tinted luster
we grew into golden suns
tart from constant heat.

1980s Specter

Wednesday Dad wore black to work,
a melancholic protest.
My parents mourned around
the dining table's privacy.
That actor would start a nuclear war.

When he joked into a mic
that missiles would launch in 2 minutes,
only I laughed it off as absurd.
Fear shrouded the community.

A science assignment to calculate
home's distance from the air force base
and the effect if nuclear warheads hit it—
designed to evaporate my optimism.
But I still thought Russians were people like me.

Southern Medusa

Kudzu hair grows rapidly over your face
twisting into a thick veil.
You have a discerning eye
practiced at viewing through foliage.
Seeing through the guise
men who can no longer gaze at you.

Southern Medusa
Safe wrapped in vines
that drain them while supporting you.

Vexing,
knots of snakes hidden within
hair takes their breath away.

Hexing,
you never have to force a smile again
the bite is sharp and fatal.

Now Ripe

Transcendent future
past ordered existence
when a complementary fruit bowl
became the sweetest bunch
needed to mature
to deepen
peel away excess flesh
same taste and manner
at the core
with proper graft
now ripe and juicy
for years of flavor

Sacral Adoptees

Outcast as prodigal.
Wandering seekers, lovers of leaving
      who struggled to unhitch your wagon from despair.

New fathers to guide to old paths.
Two decades' hard journey
      to worship your way back to old ways.

You have shed so much to lighten your load.
I see the buoyancy through your desolation.
Yet I wish you could cast off more,
      so peace could sail you through the shallows without drag.

Patron Catherine

Scholar sure
transgressed expectations
tongue turned round
pagan intellects
caressed higher love
denied any man

hagiography stripped
You remain
gendered but never conforming
uncontainable
grounded in transcendent truth.
what Wisdom
spans centuries
shared beyond space

Womyn still caress higher love
denied any man
line crossers still
gendered but never conforming
jointly possessed of transcendent truth
uncontainable, updated, timeless

Clinging Dream

Over twenty years
since the clinging dream
of an intimate house
grown strange
with buckling floors and a long hall
a basin in a sudden alcove
the feeling of teeth wiggling and falling out
was never good
but looking up to see you
made it okay
joyful closure
hair blue-tinted like yours
led by your desire
to gift me something special
into your living room
I watched from the familiar sofa
as you disappeared to the front room
returned to spill polished stones
onto the coffee table
like precious jewels
You were my last grandmother
though first to die
I returned in time
old enough to understand
that you reappeared that night
just to let me know
how long we love

Gather the Deck Again

Forever shuffling cards
in a world that separates
Kings, Queens, Jacks, Aces
although the next hand
the rabid assembly deals
is meant to make us fold.
Gather the deck again
and create a new game.
Rather than play dealer's choice
the way to happiness
out of this failed state
is lived fully as constant revolt.

Burst

Apple blossoms burst from
an ancient tree that
played dead just days ago.

Bluebonnets sprinkle the grass. Popped up from
the latest downpour.

Three friends pause at the wonder of spring blossoms
while the little dogs strain for
the next scent.

Spirit Cove

I.

The horizon
a line of light
with sun poured
onto water dispersing.

Oval glimmers tip waves
shimmer toward shore
riding in the tide
as if flashing out a message.

II.

From lookout wet rock top
light line draws the horizon into being
separates sky from sea
pours like white ink
flashes bob across wave peaks
shimmer toward shore
most capsize as the tide arrives
but the few remaining
flicker their bright message
as ocean's fireflies.

4. Part

Fly Away Dreams

Above the horizon is an altered state
   smudged with shifty clouds

      spun deceptively solid at eye level
         thickening fog ambush wipes out houses and roads.

We must rise.
The father of invention encourages me
to rest on batting spread like laurel leaves.

Swept away
eons of miles apart—

Did he dip a hand into a white mist pool
delight to hop from cloud to cloud
thrill or sober as home fell from view?

   Father left behind, invisible by design
      the comforter pierced by his alarm
         transmuting into a broken net.

Was that lolling expanse his last sight
   before a rush of air finally shook Icarus from his dreams?

Felled

What is it to be civilized
shorn from copse kin
sapling transplanted
to spread under concrete
or old pines thinned
felled by the imagined future
of them crushing the house

Fallen logs become lathe-spun art
species inlaid together
beyond habitat mingle
grains and earth born hues juxtaposed
wooden bowl gifts
hold possibilities
in negative space
warm life
against cupped hands

Vapors' Cold, Crashing Balm

Vapors' cold pulls tears to the surface
diamonds of loss frozen in place
weighing down every blade
a dazzling field in the shade

Face dawn; run burning legs to thaw
Dew evaporates in the heating day
Fog dissipates with the sunny ray
So too might grief withdraw.

Flee to the woods as balm
for stings of life disconnected from living
Rest in deep leafy soil's calm
inwardly composting forgiving

The murmur of trees above and below
connects their beings like a river's flow
urging return to the stream of relation
Yet how do we evade capsizing negation?

For now, I will dream of Ponderosas
spiraling terribly in place
tipping, crashing, crushing losses
that—even felled—retain majestic grace.

Grief Work

Although chill drizzle seeps in
can't we watch TV or dine?
I try to avert your loss
to side-step mine.

Called to do grief work better
Tell me more while I listen.
I…don't know what to say.
Windows glisten.

Some stomp grief in hot anger.
We withdraw in cold languor.

Autopsy

If I died soon
the autopsy would not reveal the real causes.
Let fire reduce the body to ash
rather than subject a corpse to restorative art.

But ask my masseuse
who remembers the tension
where muscles tried to protect trauma
Ask the dentist
who crowned teeth set on edge
ground down
Call the specialist who deadened nerves
in their wiggly tentacles
Bring in the dermatologist
to assess the rashes
where pressure erupts.

The body writes what it knows
on itself
telling the container's story
when the contents are too composed to say.

Braid: I Learned from Dementia that I Could Not Stay

Truth is a river that flows in curves;
We cannot always see around the bends,
But water will get to the bottom of things.

Water will get to the bottom of things,
And we don't have to ride each rapid down.
Drift along long enough and will feels like fate.

Freely willed choices appear fated:
Whitewater love, deep channels, muddy delta
Where live oaks spurn the river's pleas to conserve.

When roots' incursions suck the river dry,
Water retreats in calcified bands.
I learned from that hardening I could not stay.

I learned from dementia that I could not stay
In a future when I could not fend him off.
Truth is a river that flows in curves.

For Life Anew

I picture life anew
then drive to meditate
on the center line
three vultures divide a dead squirrel
I adore squirrels
but sometimes love dies
If I slow way down
will I disrupt their cleanup?
They step-flutter aside
but I know they will do their work
to sweep away detritus
for life anew

Coda:
A young squirrel attended meditation
on the fence
sitting still with us
Large black eye
met my gaze
as we ended
squirrel reached up
to chew the sapling's new buds.

Cicadas

The cicadas cry
White noise to native slumberers
Their static kept me up

At the break I flew
An epidemic kept me
North of quiet, west of serenity

Used to tornado alley
I am in the eye of the storm
Where silent devastation swirls

While cicadas crawl from dirt
And litter exoskeletons
Love blows on our fierce winds

At home among the pines

Pine Scent

Back home, pines tower over houses
live peacefully with people
unless high winds snap them
or unscrew them from the earth.

Gone for decades of tempests
I return to a lull
before a hurricane prostrates 250 trees
onto streets, power lines, houses.

The sound of chainsaws everywhere
makes pine scent unbearable
it invades my dreams
gushing sap and exhaling

the aroma of death.

Rise

Inky indigo
slowly fades
to pale cinder

Mist hangs
dripping moss draped
biomass weight
that pins limbs

As embers reignite
winds blow
flames higher
across clearing blue

If trees could shake
like dogs
they'd shoot their arms
to heaven

Flocks of birds
fire up song
a will to rise

Pine Needles Fall

pine needles fall
wind divining lottery sticks
breezy prayers
pitch incense self purifies
turns, tosses the needles
for answers
dozens scattered to the winds
a failed attempt
even when one floats down alone
two leaves follow
curled edges up
deities flat out laugh
into the breeze

From Ash

The lodgepole struck
in a flash at night
thunders as it splits
and tumbles in the bright

Kindled summer blaze
terrifies forest beasts and men
but seedlings need their ashy nurse
a forest first for them.

Babble

Babble wells up
gurgling just like
the running water
from taps
light streams down
forest bathing
still reflected
in your nature
to echo rivulets
until the sound carves
beds through your sylvan
self
little roots hold
to that ageless path
under the spring-fed canopy

5. *Every Day*

Listing Along

When the world closed in, morning's liquid gold
splashed across a wide canvas, welcoming
his return. His search turned circles,
father and son listing along the days
across the same paths to green expanses
strewn with crunching leaves that pierce the crisp air.
She fears winter nights' steeply inclined pitch
not remembering the clock's daily turn
seasons return like her repetition.
When the sky becomes water she still waves
behind cold glass zipped into her fleece
with bright eyes following her men's venture
past the unfurling crocus, shadow respites,
and shooting grass along the same old paths
spread with buds, blooms, petals, dried leaves, then ice.
And they reappear to see her again.

Reflects

Distance closed
our best self
reflects in another's pupils.
Look to see one's
self
kindled
away from
cold convention.
Open faces shine
ready to slip through
unguarded forest gateways
together.

Where Are the Squirrels?

Each night Mom picks two Brazil nuts
for Dad to set on the front stoop
as the morning ritual offering
breakfast for her drey.

We line up lunchtime peanuts
and she calls, *Where are the squirrels?*
They peer at me tentatively
then tumble over each other to reach her.

When rain puddles on the patio
she tells us birds should come drink
but no one visits
so she gazes at twin hemlocks.

Windows on the world
are better than TV.
You notice what you will
and supply the monologue.

We watch a squirrel hop, stop
front paws blur like a drill
refill over a nut so
the ground looks undisturbed.

When did you start feeding squirrels? I ask.
After I left home?

Oh sure, because you were my little squirrel.

And you have always been my oak.

To Reason with My Crooked Cap

Mornings, sleep full of cat
I stumble up
to reason with my crooked cap

Son, a ray behind a cloud
walks with Dad
through an even-tempered day

Fight to spark from boredom
a puzzle, a wonder
a way beyond naps and chocolate

Mom on repeat
They killed that Black man!
It's awful. How could they do that?
Are they in jail?
There are people in jail who shouldn't be.
They used to not let Black people vote.
They said they weren't smart enough.
You can't say that about a whole group of people!

Your compassion and
ethics still sharp
you cry out against injustice
and make sure we share equal amounts of dessert

Wintering Days

Their wintering days marked his journey
from a life crowded with people and quests
into moonlit darkness.
Cloudy nights made it hard to see ahead,
but a one-eyed Daruma wish blazed red.
Somehow, he would stay among the pine trees,
plow through the nights and snowdrifts,
scrape up dragon coins to make a soft bed.

Cloud Koan

Allow whatever thoughts arise
to come and go like clouds

a word you can't remember
the...in the sky...you know, white
some lunches the window to the world
is blue and sunny
some, *blue with...white*
some, *all white, don't like*

Stuck in rainy mud,
making bricks in the kiln
to wall away threat
builds fantasy safety
that washes away in the next rain
an eroded topsoil

Seeking answers
a vice that grips
fixed on the wrong way
looking to explain the unexplainable
instead of planting rye to hold the soil
with gentle netting.

As the seed moves earth
to root and shoot
reaching the sun
it has never seen what it
perhaps remembers
from the last generation.

Cracks

we stuff poetry
into tiny cracks
along this glacial slog
Someday
expanding crevasses
will break open
under the pressure of
our beauty
and we will slide down
shear walls to
Freedom

In Constellation

Stars long dead
gases and dust
reincarnate
as all things
including us
in nature
like clay gifted
life-giving
shape and breath.

Though things fall apart
when I feel unstable at the core
tempted to fold in on myself
collapse until insides turn to iron
know skin could crash in
to snuff out this existence

I reorient in constellation
recenter, not implode
lest the resulting black hole
suck down those closest. I
pull together a self
to fuel life
become bright.

Sounds behind the Traffic

I wake earlier than I want
to the flow of traffic
the neighbor readying for work
my companion impatient to eat
thoughts rush in
jam up

Birds chirp faintly
behind the stream of cars
mimicking the alarm that will sound
and the cat who selectively hears them
trills back.

Gray Frosted into Elegance

When hoarfrost turned all old and ashen
constant outlandish gloaming
left them heart-numb, mind-numb, soul-numb
while the cat relaxed into a fur crescent
gray frosted into elegance
like winter's colorless beauty of flora stripped away

In a world suddenly misty and chill
the twilight folks' feet shushed
past a feline's sanctum sanctorum and each other
insular natures striving to keep
from drowning in each other's tragedies.

Emotions dust the surfaces
where blood flowed when their peak collapsed
like lightening flashes image and after-image
writing the future with fire
old as my tongue

Gestures mean everything
the eruption, the wound may feel soul hurting
but shaking connection makes the you whom people believe in
the concentrated, magnified, essence of you
like formless magma transforming to basalt
like resting in the inner sanctuary on an ashy day.

Sand

fire forged into glass
to count time by grains

how the tiny boulders scratch
to escape the hourglass
break the bottom
flow back to the sea
settle beyond plumbed depths

dream cycle of longing
night ache itching to return
the grains form
re-form
pool at the corners of sleeping eyes

Nature's Shield: a protection prayer

Nature's power be our charm—
hard stone, solid Earth,
vast seas round its girth,
wind-blown cloudy whorls,
stormy thunder's roars,
the plants that ingest
life-giving sun's light,
fungi that digest
by moon and stars bright—
shield us from every harm.

Out of This World[3]

Far removed essence
shattered into torrential
monsoons crashing out
creating where it reached
ripples still
out of this world
we all come
every particle the same
all interdependent
you and I vibrate
to the same frequency
whether or not
we hear the hum.

---

[3] "You didn't come into this world. You came out of it, like a wave from the ocean. You are not a stranger here." Alan Watts, *Cloud-hidden, Whereabouts Unknown* (1973).

6. Became

Dandelion Seeds

The point
beyond time
initial unity
a dandelion
gone to seed.
Parachutes float
potential to
reconstitute
the whole.

From Greece
worldwide
sunny flowers
feed bees
ensure harvest
and healing
divine where we
have been
and will be.

Sweet Flags from Disbanded Leaves

Disbanded live oak leaves fall and desiccated moss crumbles to the ground
threaded with hot wishes he dared not speak.
As the detritus blows into the river that eventually meets the sea
waves lap at time immemorial
murmuring of ancient Greek friendship.

Nights, three mythic lovers embraced my ruddy older brother
Dionysos and a satyr turned from their rut and Herakles from clasping Antaeus.
They removed Walt's broad calico coat and open red flannel
wrestled cowhide boots from feet and blooming overalls from stout legs
until he stood with piercing wide gray eyes.

Can one strip away dandy? It clings to skin and sinew beneath casually indifferent clothes.
Older brother, show me your lazy recline with heroes, gods, and horny goats
rank sensuality and raw luxury for the masses
under loose-fitting casual wear that moves free.
Sleepy eyed, you roll a relaxed and slow soul into a quartet in crescendo.

Your loves felt your prowess in the bumps on your head.
The rough and poetic friend sticks naturally
> to handsome Irish fighters
> saucy loafers
> the big fellow in the corner
> the coarse open faced blond
> the sailor boy back from Japan
> the small gay Peter
> and the pangendered theater performer

meeting at the beer cellar, loving, sleeping with them in the great outdoors.

Walt saw Death as a beautiful youth lying with brother Sleep
wrapped together in night.
The young stiff bounds forward into dreams of unstifled love.
With Sleep, his soft comrade,
they celebrate together.

Who am I without green love
without inflamed leaves
without seasons that infatuate, abandon, accommodate, lie dormant in turn:
a bouquet of thoughts and aspirations without action,
a subject without objects or verbs,
a teacher made of patience.

I seek neither eleve nor don
but that we walk together long enough to learn each other's tender spots.
Draw up a lager with me and some heavy fare
we can work off later, free love spent at Fred Gray's.
Let's experiment with grip that is not so sticky it pastes us down.

Never oak and ivy
nor lone live oak with clinging moss
nor the sickly-sweet odor of cut flowers
but perennial sweet flag colonies wafting spicy fragrance
and waving from wet depths.

Shut Down that Winter Home

Shut down that winter home
of skin and bone
as spring ends
the cocoon suffocates
out of season

Your waning moon
cannot cast the light
and warmth you need
to brighten this scene

Don't wait

There is no better
tomorrow here
no homecoming
but beyond all this

Board up what
in disarray
keeps you from the sun
exchange drear for
purified light

Where a summer honeymoon awaits

Open to a new world
where two and one
need not abrade as three

Where fulfilled from joyful naming
the self works high diplomacy
and attains transformation

Your world is not here
amid rotting ephemera and piss
or fluorescent beeps

Dance naked crowned in laurel
as you accept cosmic consciousness
the prize at the end of the race

Everything gone so terribly wrong
will fall away
past purged with perspective

Flames scorch earth
before eucalyptus pop open
before fireweed reappears

To reseed interdependence
that buried shell of talent
dissolves to bloom into creativity

Cobalt Night Skies

Cobalt night skies crowd out days
as charcoal silhouette trees
stand sentinels that urge
slow down, rest
sleep warm within our circle
dark hours extend
hibernation's calls

Moon lights
the few steps to a cement clearing
Sage invites four directions
acolytes turn in time
light wreath upon wreath past
dry brittle kindling flames high
flickering Rorschach

Each year ashes
may smoke smudge long night
to purify daybreak
as past smolders
she asks the North to look over us
that ash beget
new growth

Days' short brilliance
fiery pages fall red, orange, yellow
extinguish on the grass
that I rolled over
in spontaneous joy
my prayer a hope
a gathering in the den
to nourish family
through cold cobalt night skies

Hindsight Rebirthing

All those generations beat drums
to drive away the longest night
stave off feared death
and revive growing days

But the yearly cycle means
the old year is dying to be reborn
It has aged into sleeping more
lengthening nights

Braid: He Wears Woods

He wears woods as a guided meditation,
His back against the silver orange bark.
Here now, but sensing the roaring river.

Hear now the roaring river on him
That Hokusai blue, aqua, and white
Runs by a path worn through the understory.

A path gleams along the forest floor
Of river stones further smoothed by saunters,
Stippled with needles from regal pines.

Nature's majestic Ponderosas
Have thinned in winds and the onslaught of saws
Yet they mark the land as much as basalt.

They mark the land as much as native rock;
In his childhood and through the ages
He wears woods as a guided meditation.

Insecurely Tethered

Frost has turned her mind
but darkened her hair
so she cannot remember her age
and doesn't look it

Mist freezes on the glass table
she cleans obsessively
tidying outdoors
while she notices internal disorder

Groping for words
making up motives
revising histories far from fact
all standard deviations

Only significant by degrees

Fewer filters
less care for appearance
could be eccentric
like wearing purple with red

But everything is boring
when hearing is impoverished
processing gone
little entertains

What are we
sans memory
in the grip
of sleep grit

Not knowing where we are

The world grows chilly
as she sleeps more and more
waiting to eat, to sit together

never quite believing she got dessert

The loss of former joys
with no replacements
no longer able to
read, play cards, follow dialogue

Inability to reach joy disables

Still eyes clear
feeling strong
of right and wrong
ethics here and holding dear

Before we pass
we forget to talk
to eat, to walk
but in twilight a core remains

Insecurely tethered to the past

Chants All Over

Heroic is the ant
and worker bee
crocus and crab apple tree
the Everyman
in me

The mockingbird
chants so complicated
then dive bombs
women walking dogs
'til sinful thoughts arise
of strangling songbirds

You can find the key
of cat's meow
on the piano
or guitar string
plucked to choke the chicken

When waves of peeper trills
subside
they go gently
and the pond is still
for what? everything to come

Rest your head on me
involuntary murmurs
lull us
rocked on their waves
to sleep

Make My Man Basalt

Waterlogged clay
slippery muddy creation
makes for shifty boys

Make my man basalt
crack oozing magma
cools dark, porous
a solid column of a guy

The Art of Dying

Fallen brethren sheltered green men removed to towns.
Old growth woods reborn as birthing stools and beds
   to usher in new life,
     finally carried artisans to their graves.
What, so thickly leafed, filtered out most light,
   now buffeted copses.
Premodernists were more artful than efficient.

Their pulped, long dusty leaves prescribed the good death
   that follows plenty of time for reflection
   and reconciliation with the Sender.
The medieval mind abhorred a quick death.

Elder brothers and uncles who survived bashings and plague
   know the perils of a fast, sure, violent wasting.
In the postindustrial age, though,
   where yours and mine have decades to ruminate,
   I sigh relief when elders die in bed at home.

Transplanted maple, so well-grafted
   that one half could not live a year beyond the other,
   still flourished twice as long as old-world counterparts.
So too the tulip poplar,
   grown to build and cut down at 66 rings.
Bald cypress finally not waking to cold dread.
Magnolia, sturdy as steel, succumbing at last.
Then the drier pine.
Driftwood marks the carver's passing.

A fallen California bay laurel crowns this extended family,
   together a rare quarto about
   a new good death

—old, in bed, at home, surrounded by love—

in an age when machines press the body of work beyond its time
and alienate the falling leaves from the roots they would nourish.

Braid: Shrinking

I sink into warm water tonight,
Shrink by crossing legs, so I can float.
Is this how it feels to bob unmoored from names?

She floats in a lake unmoored from names;
Mine drifted away, so she cannot say
How we are related except I am "special."

We are related; accept I am special
Like cake, GU basketball, I don't know what;
The unsure word means rare and great.

The uncertain word for rare and great
Covers specifics we cannot guess,
Swims in an evaporating pool.

Swimming in an evaporating pool
Tonight I add salt to the water
As I sink into its warm embrace.

Fireweed

How fast they return, witness the certain
Rhizomes regenerate green shoots
Surface through scorched earth
In a month
A cluster of life.

Smooth willow-shaped leaves
Emerald to the sun, silver to the earth
Deer eat the slippery spinach.
When stalks age
Children scoop out the pith
As a sweet treat.
Mothers thicken soups.

Four-petal fuchsia blooms
Low on the stem.
Women who brew leaves
As a berry citrus tea
Steep calm from wildfires.

When fireweed fruits release
Hundreds of tufted seeds
To the winds
Each feathery puff insists on life
After catastrophe.

Every Day, They Became Part of Him

The sight of buds
unfurled day after day
until he saw them at night
flashes on his eyelid screen
real as soft petals

The tang of apples
swelled his cheeks
and belly
made him glean more
and wait for top picks to fall

The crunch of leaves
entered him
sound waves
reverberated through his soles
splashed in his ears

The smell of pine
wafted molecules
blended and changed places
with him
until he huffed sprigs daily

The man beside him
shaped him
gave him himself
walked away and back to her
and "every day, they became part of him."[4]

---

[4] Line from Walt Whitman, "There was a Child Went Forth," *The Complete Poems of Walt Whitman* (Ware, Hertfordshire, England: Wordsworth Poetry Library, 1995), 274.

Clark A. Pomerleau grew up in Spokane, Washington. There, beauty merges indigenous rock and trees with managed nature; basalt juts from lawns and ponderosa pines populate the edges of the Nishinomiya Tsutakawa Japanese Garden. Likewise, Pomerleau's writing joins forms not always in association. His academic and diversity inclusion publications emerged as a symbiosis of oral history and intersectional feminism. Storying expands in his chapbook (*Better Living through Cats,*) and this, his first full-length poetry book, to consider how blending experience with dreams points toward greater truths. Influenced by queer, trans, environmental, and disability studies, Pomerleau's poems seek fusions that disrupt normative divisions. To that end, *Every Day, They Became Part of Him* is part autobiography, part Everygenderqueer (to update the "Everyman" archetype). Engaging with family, nature, histories of oppression, and spirituality, the poems share experiences along with concerns and questions. Pomerleau draws readers into a poetic space that asks: How do we integrate celebrations of resistance, conflicting desires, and lessons from other beings? How do we foster relationship in the moment with a loved one whose situated reality does not conform to normative views of time? How can we preserve our sense of wonder?

www.ingramcontent.com/pod-product-compliance
Lightning Source LLC
Chambersburg PA
CBHW020857160426
43192CB00007B/969